50 Hawaiian Island Cuisine at Home

By: Kelly Johnson

Table of Contents

- Huli Huli Chicken
- Poke Bowl with Ahi Tuna
- Loco Moco
- Hawaiian BBQ Ribs
- Spam Musubi
- Kalua Pork
- Shoyu Chicken
- Mahi-Mahi Tacos
- Coconut Shrimp
- Haupia (Coconut Pudding)
- Ahi Poke with Soy Sauce and Sesame
- Hawaiian Style Macaroni Salad
- Pineapple Fried Rice
- Island-Style Beef Stew
- Sweet and Sour Chicken
- Grilled Teriyaki Chicken
- Poi (Taro Paste)
- Mango Shrimp Ceviche
- Taro Chips with Mango Salsa
- Hawaiian-Style Sweet Potatoes
- Pina Colada Smoothie
- Coconut Rice
- Kalbi Ribs
- Luau-Style Chicken
- Pineapple Glazed Ham
- Island-Style Grilled Fish
- Chicken Long Rice
- Fish Tacos with Mango Salsa
- Ahi Poke with Avocado
- Coconut-Crusted Fish
- Pineapple Upside-Down Cake
- Island-Style Sweet and Spicy Shrimp
- Saimin (Hawaiian Noodle Soup)
- Chicken Katsu
- Hoisin-Glazed Grilled Pork

- Hawaiian-Style Pork Tacos
- Grilled Mahi-Mahi with Pineapple Salsa
- Tropical Fruit Salad
- Coconut-Lime Chicken
- Hawaiian Ahi Tuna Tartare
- Lomi Lomi Salmon
- Macadamia Nut Crusted Fish
- Haupia Pie
- Kona Coffee Rubbed Steak
- Spam and Egg Breakfast Sandwich
- Hawaiian Luau Pork Sliders
- Poke Nachos
- Papaya Salad
- Sweet Potato Coconut Casserole
- Ulu (Breadfruit) Salad

Huli Huli Chicken

Ingredients:

- 4 chicken breasts
- 1/2 cup soy sauce
- 1/4 cup ketchup
- 1/4 cup brown sugar
- 1/4 cup pineapple juice
- 2 cloves garlic, minced
- 1-inch piece of ginger, grated
- 2 tbsp rice vinegar
- 1 tbsp sesame oil

Instructions:

1. **Marinate the Chicken**: Mix soy sauce, ketchup, brown sugar, pineapple juice, garlic, ginger, rice vinegar, and sesame oil in a bowl. Pour over the chicken and refrigerate for 2 hours or overnight.
2. **Grill the Chicken**: Preheat grill to medium-high heat. Grill the chicken for 6-8 minutes on each side, brushing with marinade during grilling.
3. **Serve**: Slice and serve with rice and grilled vegetables.

Poke Bowl with Ahi Tuna

Ingredients:

- 1 lb Ahi tuna, cubed
- 2 tbsp soy sauce
- 1 tbsp sesame oil
- 1 tsp rice vinegar
- 1 tsp honey
- 1/2 tsp chili flakes
- 1 avocado, sliced
- 1/4 cucumber, sliced
- 1/4 cup edamame
- 1 cup cooked sushi rice
- 1 tbsp toasted sesame seeds

Instructions:

1. **Prepare Tuna**: In a bowl, combine soy sauce, sesame oil, rice vinegar, honey, and chili flakes. Add tuna cubes and mix gently.
2. **Assemble the Bowl**: Place a serving of sushi rice in a bowl. Arrange marinated tuna, avocado, cucumber, edamame, and sesame seeds on top.
3. **Serve**: Drizzle with extra sauce and serve immediately.

Loco Moco

Ingredients:

- 2 cups cooked white rice
- 4 beef patties
- 2 eggs
- 1/4 cup soy sauce
- 1/4 cup beef broth
- 2 tbsp cornstarch
- 1/2 cup onions, diced
- 2 tbsp butter

Instructions:

1. **Cook Beef Patties**: Cook beef patties in a skillet over medium heat until browned and cooked through. Set aside.
2. **Make Gravy**: In the same skillet, melt butter and sauté onions until softened. Add soy sauce and beef broth. Bring to a simmer and thicken with cornstarch mixed with water.
3. **Assemble the Loco Moco**: Place a scoop of rice on each plate. Top with a beef patty, a fried egg, and pour the gravy over the top. Serve immediately.

Hawaiian BBQ Ribs

Ingredients:

- 2 racks of baby back ribs
- 1/4 cup soy sauce
- 1/4 cup brown sugar
- 1/4 cup pineapple juice
- 2 tbsp hoisin sauce
- 2 tbsp rice vinegar
- 1 tbsp garlic, minced
- 1 tbsp ginger, minced
- 1 tbsp sesame oil

Instructions:

1. **Preheat Oven**: Preheat the oven to 300°F (150°C).
2. **Prepare Ribs**: Remove the membrane from the back of the ribs. Mix soy sauce, brown sugar, pineapple juice, hoisin sauce, rice vinegar, garlic, ginger, and sesame oil in a bowl. Brush the ribs with the sauce.
3. **Bake**: Place ribs on a baking sheet and cover with foil. Bake for 2.5-3 hours, basting with the sauce every 30 minutes.
4. **Finish on Grill**: Preheat grill to medium-high heat. Grill ribs for 5-10 minutes, brushing with sauce, until caramelized. Serve with extra sauce.

Spam Musubi

Ingredients:

- 1 can Spam, sliced into 8 pieces
- 2 cups cooked sushi rice
- 2 tbsp soy sauce
- 1 tbsp rice vinegar
- 1 tbsp sugar
- 8 sheets nori (seaweed)

Instructions:

1. **Cook Spam**: Sauté the Spam slices in a skillet over medium heat until browned on both sides.
2. **Prepare Rice**: Mix soy sauce, rice vinegar, and sugar in a small bowl. Gently fold this mixture into the warm rice.
3. **Assemble Musubi**: Place a sheet of nori on a clean surface. Mold a scoop of rice into a rectangle and place a slice of Spam on top. Roll up tightly and seal with a bit of water. Repeat with remaining ingredients.

Kalua Pork

Ingredients:

- 4 lbs pork shoulder
- 1 tbsp Hawaiian sea salt
- 1 tbsp liquid smoke

Instructions:

1. **Prepare Pork**: Rub the pork shoulder with sea salt and liquid smoke.
2. **Slow Cook**: Place in a slow cooker and cook on low for 8 hours until the pork is tender and easily shredded.
3. **Shred and Serve**: Shred the pork and serve with rice and vegetables.

Shoyu Chicken

Ingredients:

- 4 chicken thighs
- 1/2 cup soy sauce
- 1/4 cup brown sugar
- 1/4 cup water
- 2 cloves garlic, minced
- 1-inch piece of ginger, sliced

Instructions:

1. **Make Sauce**: In a pot, combine soy sauce, brown sugar, water, garlic, and ginger. Bring to a simmer until sugar dissolves.
2. **Cook Chicken**: Place chicken thighs in a large pan and pour the sauce over the top. Simmer for 25-30 minutes until chicken is cooked through.
3. **Serve**: Serve over rice with steamed vegetables.

Mahi-Mahi Tacos

Ingredients:

- 4 mahi-mahi fillets
- 1 tbsp olive oil
- 1/2 tsp cumin
- 1/2 tsp chili powder
- 1/4 tsp garlic powder
- 1/4 tsp salt
- 8 small corn tortillas
- 1/2 cup cabbage, shredded
- 1/4 cup cilantro, chopped
- 1 lime, cut into wedges

Instructions:

1. **Cook Fish**: Season mahi-mahi fillets with olive oil, cumin, chili powder, garlic powder, and salt. Grill or pan-fry for 3-4 minutes per side until cooked through.
2. **Assemble Tacos**: Warm tortillas and top with cooked mahi-mahi, shredded cabbage, cilantro, and a squeeze of lime.
3. **Serve**: Serve immediately with extra lime wedges on the side.

Coconut Shrimp

Ingredients:

- 1 lb large shrimp, peeled and deveined
- 1/2 cup all-purpose flour
- 1/2 tsp salt
- 1/2 tsp black pepper
- 2 large eggs, beaten
- 1 cup shredded coconut
- 1/2 cup panko breadcrumbs
- Vegetable oil for frying

Instructions:

1. **Prepare Breading**: In a shallow dish, combine flour, salt, and pepper. In another dish, beat the eggs. In a third dish, mix shredded coconut and panko breadcrumbs.
2. **Coat Shrimp**: Dredge each shrimp in the flour mixture, dip into the egg, and then coat with the coconut-panko mixture.
3. **Fry Shrimp**: Heat oil in a large skillet over medium-high heat. Fry shrimp in batches for 2-3 minutes per side until golden brown.
4. **Serve**: Serve with sweet chili sauce or pineapple salsa.

Haupia (Coconut Pudding)

Ingredients:

- 1 can (13.5 oz) coconut milk
- 1/2 cup whole milk
- 1/2 cup sugar
- 1/4 cup cornstarch
- Pinch of salt

Instructions:

1. **Combine Ingredients**: In a medium saucepan, whisk together coconut milk, whole milk, sugar, cornstarch, and salt.
2. **Cook the Pudding**: Place the saucepan over medium heat and cook, whisking constantly, until the mixture thickens (about 5-7 minutes).
3. **Chill**: Pour the pudding into a dish or individual cups and refrigerate for at least 2 hours, or until set.
4. **Serve**: Serve chilled with toasted coconut flakes on top, if desired.

Ahi Poke with Soy Sauce and Sesame

Ingredients:

- 1 lb fresh ahi tuna, cubed
- 1/4 cup soy sauce
- 1 tbsp sesame oil
- 1 tbsp rice vinegar
- 1/2 tsp chili flakes
- 2 tbsp green onions, sliced
- 1 tbsp toasted sesame seeds

Instructions:

1. **Prepare Tuna**: Place the cubed ahi tuna in a bowl.
2. **Make Sauce**: In a small bowl, combine soy sauce, sesame oil, rice vinegar, and chili flakes.
3. **Mix**: Pour the sauce over the tuna and toss gently to combine.
4. **Serve**: Top with sliced green onions and toasted sesame seeds. Serve with rice or as an appetizer.

Hawaiian Style Macaroni Salad

Ingredients:

- 2 cups elbow macaroni, cooked
- 1/2 cup mayonnaise
- 1/4 cup apple cider vinegar
- 2 tbsp sugar
- 1/2 cup grated carrots
- 1/4 cup diced celery
- 1/4 cup green onions, chopped
- Salt and pepper to taste

Instructions:

1. **Combine Ingredients**: In a large bowl, combine cooked macaroni, mayonnaise, vinegar, and sugar.
2. **Add Vegetables**: Stir in grated carrots, diced celery, and chopped green onions.
3. **Season**: Add salt and pepper to taste.
4. **Chill and Serve**: Refrigerate for at least 1 hour before serving to allow flavors to meld.

Pineapple Fried Rice

Ingredients:

- 2 cups cooked jasmine rice (preferably day-old)
- 1 tbsp vegetable oil
- 1/2 cup diced onion
- 1/2 cup diced bell pepper
- 1/2 cup pineapple chunks
- 1/4 cup frozen peas
- 2 eggs, scrambled
- 2 tbsp soy sauce
- 1 tbsp oyster sauce
- 1/2 tsp sesame oil
- 2 tbsp chopped green onions
  Instructions:

1. **Prepare Vegetables**: Heat vegetable oil in a large pan over medium heat. Add onion and bell pepper and cook until softened.
2. **Cook Rice**: Add pineapple chunks and peas, and cook for another 2 minutes. Push the veggies to the side of the pan and scramble the eggs in the empty space.
3. **Combine and Season**: Add the rice to the pan and stir to combine with the vegetables and eggs. Add soy sauce, oyster sauce, and sesame oil, and stir-fry for 3-4 minutes.
4. **Finish**: Garnish with chopped green onions and serve.

Island-Style Beef Stew

Ingredients:

- 2 lbs beef stew meat, cubed
- 1/2 cup soy sauce
- 1/4 cup brown sugar
- 4 cups beef broth
- 3 cloves garlic, minced
- 1 onion, chopped
- 2 carrots, sliced
- 2 potatoes, diced
- 1/2 tsp ground ginger
- Salt and pepper to taste

Instructions:

1. **Brown the Beef**: In a large pot, brown the beef stew meat on all sides.
2. **Cook Aromatics**: Add garlic, onion, and ginger, cooking until fragrant.
3. **Simmer**: Add soy sauce, brown sugar, beef broth, carrots, and potatoes. Bring to a simmer and cook for 1.5-2 hours until beef is tender.
4. **Season and Serve**: Season with salt and pepper to taste, and serve with rice or crusty bread.

Sweet and Sour Chicken

Ingredients:

- 1 lb chicken breast, cubed
- 1/4 cup cornstarch
- 1/4 cup vegetable oil
- 1/2 cup pineapple juice
- 1/4 cup vinegar
- 1/4 cup ketchup
- 1/4 cup sugar
- 1 tbsp soy sauce
- 1 bell pepper, chopped
- 1/2 onion, chopped
- Pineapple chunks

Instructions:

1. **Coat the Chicken**: Coat the chicken cubes in cornstarch.
2. **Fry Chicken**: Heat vegetable oil in a large pan and fry the chicken until golden brown. Remove and set aside.
3. **Make Sauce**: In a separate pan, combine pineapple juice, vinegar, ketchup, sugar, and soy sauce. Bring to a boil, then reduce to simmer.
4. **Combine**: Add the fried chicken, bell pepper, onion, and pineapple chunks to the sauce. Stir until the sauce thickens and coats the chicken.
5. **Serve**: Serve over rice.

Grilled Teriyaki Chicken

Ingredients:

- 4 chicken breasts
- 1/4 cup soy sauce
- 1/4 cup honey
- 2 tbsp rice vinegar
- 2 tbsp sesame oil
- 2 cloves garlic, minced
- 1 tbsp grated ginger

Instructions:

1. **Prepare Marinade**: In a bowl, whisk together soy sauce, honey, rice vinegar, sesame oil, garlic, and ginger.
2. **Marinate Chicken**: Place chicken breasts in the marinade and refrigerate for at least 2 hours.
3. **Grill**: Preheat the grill to medium-high heat. Grill chicken for 6-7 minutes per side until cooked through.
4. **Serve**: Serve with grilled vegetables or rice.

Poi (Taro Paste)

Ingredients:

- 2 lbs taro root
- Water
- Salt to taste

Instructions:

1. **Prepare Taro**: Peel the taro root and cut it into cubes.
2. **Cook Taro**: Place the cubed taro in a pot of water and bring to a boil. Cook for about 45 minutes, or until the taro is fork-tender.
3. **Mash Taro**: Drain the water and mash the taro with a pestle or potato masher until smooth. Add water to adjust the consistency to your liking. Season with salt.
4. **Serve**: Serve poi as a traditional side dish, often enjoyed with fish or pork.

Mango Shrimp Ceviche

Ingredients:

- 1 lb cooked shrimp, peeled and chopped
- 1 ripe mango, diced
- 1/4 cup red onion, finely chopped
- 1/4 cup cilantro, chopped
- 1-2 jalapeños, minced (optional)
- Juice of 2 limes
- Salt and pepper to taste

Instructions:

1. **Combine Ingredients**: In a large bowl, combine the shrimp, mango, red onion, cilantro, and jalapeños.
2. **Season**: Add the lime juice and toss to coat. Season with salt and pepper.
3. **Chill**: Refrigerate for at least 30 minutes to let the flavors meld.
4. **Serve**: Serve chilled with tortilla chips or as a side dish.

Taro Chips with Mango Salsa

Ingredients:

- 2 medium taro roots, peeled and thinly sliced
- Vegetable oil for frying
- Salt to taste
  For the Mango Salsa:
- 1 ripe mango, diced
- 1/4 cup red onion, finely chopped
- 1/4 cup cilantro, chopped
- 1 jalapeño, minced (optional)
- Juice of 1 lime
- Salt to taste
  Instructions:

1. **Make Taro Chips**: Heat oil in a deep pan to 350°F (175°C). Fry the thinly sliced taro chips in batches until golden and crispy. Drain on paper towels and season with salt.
2. **Prepare Mango Salsa**: In a bowl, combine the mango, red onion, cilantro, jalapeño, and lime juice. Season with salt to taste.
3. **Serve**: Serve the taro chips with mango salsa on the side for dipping.

Hawaiian-Style Sweet Potatoes

Ingredients:

- 4 medium sweet potatoes, peeled and cubed
- 1 tbsp olive oil
- 1 tsp cinnamon
- 1/2 tsp nutmeg
- 1/4 cup honey
- 1/4 cup coconut milk
- Salt to taste

Instructions:

1. **Roast Sweet Potatoes**: Preheat the oven to 400°F (200°C). Toss the cubed sweet potatoes in olive oil, cinnamon, and nutmeg. Spread them in a single layer on a baking sheet and roast for 25-30 minutes until tender.
2. **Prepare Sauce**: In a small saucepan, heat honey and coconut milk together until warmed.
3. **Combine**: Drizzle the honey-coconut sauce over the roasted sweet potatoes. Toss gently to coat.
4. **Serve**: Serve as a sweet and savory side dish.

Pina Colada Smoothie

Ingredients:

- 1 cup pineapple chunks
- 1/2 cup coconut milk
- 1/2 cup Greek yogurt
- 1/2 cup ice cubes
- 1 tbsp honey or agave syrup

Instructions:

1. **Blend Ingredients**: Add pineapple, coconut milk, Greek yogurt, ice, and honey to a blender.
2. **Blend**: Blend until smooth and creamy.
3. **Serve**: Pour into glasses and serve immediately, garnished with a pineapple wedge or a maraschino cherry.

Coconut Rice

Ingredients:

- 2 cups jasmine rice
- 1 can (13.5 oz) coconut milk
- 1 cup water
- 1/2 tsp salt

Instructions:

1. **Rinse Rice**: Rinse the rice under cold water until the water runs clear.
2. **Cook Rice**: In a pot, combine coconut milk, water, salt, and rinsed rice. Bring to a boil.
3. **Simmer**: Once boiling, reduce heat to low, cover, and simmer for 18-20 minutes, until the rice is tender and the liquid is absorbed.
4. **Fluff and Serve**: Fluff the rice with a fork before serving.

Kalbi Ribs

Ingredients:

- 2 lbs beef short ribs (flanken cut)
- 1/4 cup soy sauce
- 1/4 cup brown sugar
- 1/4 cup sesame oil
- 4 cloves garlic, minced
- 2 tbsp grated ginger
- 1 tbsp rice vinegar
- 2 tbsp green onions, chopped
- 1 tbsp sesame seeds

Instructions:

1. **Marinate Ribs**: In a bowl, combine soy sauce, brown sugar, sesame oil, garlic, ginger, and rice vinegar. Place the ribs in a zip-top bag and pour the marinade over the meat. Seal and refrigerate for 4-6 hours, or overnight.
2. **Grill Ribs**: Preheat the grill to medium-high heat. Grill the ribs for 3-4 minutes per side, until they're caramelized and slightly charred.
3. **Serve**: Garnish with green onions and sesame seeds before serving.

Luau-Style Chicken

Ingredients:

- 4 chicken breasts or thighs
- 1/4 cup soy sauce
- 1/4 cup pineapple juice
- 2 tbsp brown sugar
- 2 tbsp olive oil
- 2 cloves garlic, minced
- 1 tbsp grated ginger
- 1/4 cup green onions, chopped

Instructions:

1. **Marinate Chicken**: In a bowl, whisk together soy sauce, pineapple juice, brown sugar, olive oil, garlic, and ginger. Marinate the chicken for at least 2 hours.
2. **Cook Chicken**: Preheat the grill or a skillet to medium heat. Grill or cook the chicken for 6-7 minutes per side, until cooked through.
3. **Serve**: Garnish with chopped green onions and serve with steamed rice or a side salad.

Pineapple Glazed Ham

Ingredients:

- 1 (6-8 lbs) ham
- 1 cup pineapple juice
- 1/2 cup brown sugar
- 1/4 cup Dijon mustard
- 1/4 cup honey
- 1 tbsp cornstarch (optional, for thickening)

Instructions:

1. **Prepare the Ham**: Preheat the oven to 325°F (165°C). Score the surface of the ham in a diamond pattern.
2. **Make the Glaze**: In a saucepan, combine pineapple juice, brown sugar, Dijon mustard, and honey. Bring to a simmer over medium heat, stirring occasionally. Simmer for 10-15 minutes. If you prefer a thicker glaze, mix cornstarch with a little water and stir into the glaze to thicken.
3. **Bake the Ham**: Place the ham in a roasting pan and brush with the glaze. Roast for 1.5 to 2 hours, basting the ham with the glaze every 20 minutes until caramelized.
4. **Serve**: Slice the ham and drizzle with remaining glaze before serving.

Island-Style Grilled Fish

Ingredients:

- 4 fish fillets (snapper, mahi-mahi, or your choice)
- 2 tbsp olive oil
- 2 tbsp fresh lime juice
- 1 tbsp soy sauce
- 2 cloves garlic, minced
- 1 tsp paprika
- Salt and pepper to taste

Instructions:

1. **Marinate the Fish**: In a small bowl, combine olive oil, lime juice, soy sauce, garlic, paprika, salt, and pepper. Coat the fish fillets with the marinade and let them sit for 15-30 minutes.
2. **Grill the Fish**: Preheat the grill to medium heat. Grill the fish for about 4-5 minutes per side, depending on thickness, until the fish is cooked through and flakes easily.
3. **Serve**: Serve the grilled fish with rice, grilled vegetables, or a tropical fruit salad.

Chicken Long Rice

Ingredients:

- 1 lb chicken thighs, bone-in, skinless
- 6 cups chicken broth
- 2 oz dried long rice (or Chinese cellophane noodles)
- 2 tbsp soy sauce
- 2 cloves garlic, minced
- 1 inch ginger, grated
- 1/4 cup green onions, chopped
- Salt and pepper to taste

Instructions:

1. **Cook Chicken**: In a large pot, bring the chicken broth to a boil. Add the chicken thighs, soy sauce, garlic, and ginger. Simmer for 30-40 minutes until the chicken is tender and cooked through.
2. **Prepare Long Rice**: While the chicken cooks, soak the dried long rice in warm water for 10 minutes, then drain.
3. **Shred Chicken**: Remove the chicken from the broth and shred the meat using two forks.
4. **Combine**: Add the long rice to the broth and cook for an additional 10-15 minutes until the rice is tender. Return the shredded chicken to the pot and simmer for a few more minutes.
5. **Serve**: Garnish with chopped green onions before serving.

Fish Tacos with Mango Salsa

Ingredients:

- 4 fish fillets (tilapia, cod, or mahi-mahi)
- 1 tbsp olive oil
- 1 tsp cumin
- 1 tsp paprika
- Salt and pepper to taste
- 8 small corn tortillas
  For the Mango Salsa:
- 1 ripe mango, diced
- 1/4 cup red onion, finely chopped
- 1/4 cup cilantro, chopped
- 1 jalapeño, minced (optional)
- Juice of 1 lime
- Salt to taste

Instructions:

1. **Prepare the Fish**: Season the fish fillets with olive oil, cumin, paprika, salt, and pepper. Grill or pan-fry the fillets for about 3-4 minutes per side until cooked through.
2. **Make the Mango Salsa**: In a bowl, combine mango, red onion, cilantro, jalapeño, lime juice, and salt.
3. **Assemble the Tacos**: Warm the corn tortillas on a skillet. Flake the cooked fish onto each tortilla and top with the mango salsa.
4. **Serve**: Serve immediately with a side of lime wedges.

Ahi Poke with Avocado

Ingredients:

- 1 lb fresh ahi tuna, diced into cubes
- 1/4 cup soy sauce
- 1 tbsp sesame oil
- 1 tbsp rice vinegar
- 1 tsp grated ginger
- 1 avocado, diced
- 2 tbsp green onions, chopped
- 1 tbsp sesame seeds

Instructions:

1. **Prepare the Tuna**: In a bowl, combine soy sauce, sesame oil, rice vinegar, and ginger. Add the diced tuna and toss gently to coat. Let it marinate for 15 minutes.
2. **Add Avocado**: Carefully fold in the diced avocado and green onions.
3. **Serve**: Garnish with sesame seeds before serving. Serve as an appetizer or a light meal.

Coconut-Crusted Fish

Ingredients:

- 4 fish fillets (cod, tilapia, or mahi-mahi)
- 1/2 cup shredded coconut
- 1/4 cup breadcrumbs
- 1/4 cup flour
- 2 eggs, beaten
- Salt and pepper to taste
- Vegetable oil for frying

Instructions:

1. **Prepare Coating**: In one bowl, combine shredded coconut, breadcrumbs, salt, and pepper. In a separate bowl, place the flour. In another bowl, beat the eggs.
2. **Coat the Fish**: Dredge each fish fillet in the flour, dip into the egg, and coat with the coconut-breadcrumb mixture.
3. **Fry the Fish**: Heat oil in a skillet over medium heat. Fry the coated fish fillets for 4-5 minutes per side, until golden brown and cooked through.
4. **Serve**: Serve with a squeeze of fresh lime and a side of rice or salad.

Pineapple Upside-Down Cake

Ingredients:

- 1 can (20 oz) pineapple slices, drained
- 1/2 cup brown sugar
- 1/4 cup butter
- 1 box yellow cake mix (plus ingredients to prepare)
- Maraschino cherries (optional)

Instructions:

1. **Prepare the Topping**: Preheat the oven to 350°F (175°C). In a skillet, melt butter and brown sugar over medium heat until bubbling. Arrange the pineapple slices in the skillet, and place cherries in the center of each slice.
2. **Make the Cake**: Prepare the cake mix according to the package instructions. Pour the batter over the pineapple and sugar mixture.
3. **Bake**: Bake for 30-35 minutes, or until a toothpick inserted in the center comes out clean.
4. **Invert and Serve**: Let the cake cool for 5 minutes, then invert onto a plate to reveal the caramelized pineapple topping.

Island-Style Sweet and Spicy Shrimp

Ingredients:

- 1 lb shrimp, peeled and deveined
- 2 tbsp olive oil
- 2 tbsp honey
- 1 tbsp soy sauce
- 1 tsp sriracha sauce (or to taste)
- 1/2 tsp garlic powder
- 1/4 tsp cayenne pepper
- 2 tbsp green onions, chopped

Instructions:

1. **Prepare the Sauce**: In a small bowl, mix together olive oil, honey, soy sauce, sriracha, garlic powder, and cayenne pepper.
2. **Cook the Shrimp**: Heat a skillet over medium-high heat. Add the shrimp and cook for 2-3 minutes per side until pink and cooked through.
3. **Toss in Sauce**: Add the sauce to the skillet and toss the shrimp to coat evenly. Cook for another 1-2 minutes to let the sauce thicken.
4. **Serve**: Garnish with chopped green onions and serve with rice or vegetables.

Saimin (Hawaiian Noodle Soup)

Ingredients:

- 4 cups chicken broth
- 2 cups dashi (Japanese fish stock)
- 1/2 lb pork belly, thinly sliced
- 1/2 lb fresh saimin noodles (or ramen noodles)
- 2 tbsp soy sauce
- 1 tbsp sesame oil
- 1 tbsp sugar
- 2 boiled eggs, halved
- 1/4 cup green onions, chopped
- 1/4 cup nori (seaweed), shredded
- 1/4 cup kamaboko (fish cake), sliced
- 1 tsp sesame seeds

Instructions:

1. **Prepare Broth**: In a large pot, combine chicken broth and dashi. Bring to a simmer over medium heat and cook for 10 minutes. Add soy sauce, sesame oil, and sugar, stirring to combine.
2. **Cook Noodles**: Cook the saimin noodles according to package instructions, then drain.
3. **Assemble Soup**: Divide the noodles into bowls. Pour the broth over the noodles, and top with sliced pork belly, boiled eggs, green onions, nori, kamaboko, and sesame seeds.
4. **Serve**: Serve hot, garnished with additional green onions if desired.

Chicken Katsu

Ingredients:

- 4 boneless, skinless chicken breasts
- 1 cup panko breadcrumbs
- 1/2 cup all-purpose flour
- 2 eggs, beaten
- 1 tsp garlic powder
- 1 tsp onion powder
- Salt and pepper to taste
- Vegetable oil for frying

Instructions:

1. **Prepare the Chicken**: Flatten the chicken breasts to an even thickness by gently pounding with a meat mallet. Season with salt and pepper.
2. **Bread the Chicken**: Set up a breading station: place flour in one shallow dish, beaten eggs in another, and panko breadcrumbs in a third. Dredge each chicken breast in flour, dip in eggs, and coat with panko breadcrumbs.
3. **Fry the Chicken**: Heat oil in a large skillet over medium heat. Fry the chicken for about 4-5 minutes per side, or until golden brown and cooked through.
4. **Serve**: Serve the chicken katsu with a side of rice and drizzle with tonkatsu sauce or your favorite dipping sauce.

Hoisin-Glazed Grilled Pork

Ingredients:

- 1 lb pork tenderloin or pork chops
- 3 tbsp hoisin sauce
- 2 tbsp soy sauce
- 1 tbsp rice vinegar
- 1 tbsp honey
- 1 tbsp grated ginger
- 2 cloves garlic, minced
- 1 tsp sesame oil
- 1/4 tsp five-spice powder

Instructions:

1. **Prepare the Marinade**: In a bowl, combine hoisin sauce, soy sauce, rice vinegar, honey, ginger, garlic, sesame oil, and five-spice powder.
2. **Marinate the Pork**: Place the pork in a shallow dish or resealable bag and pour the marinade over it. Let it marinate for at least 1 hour, preferably overnight.
3. **Grill the Pork**: Preheat the grill to medium-high heat. Grill the pork for 4-5 minutes per side, or until it reaches an internal temperature of 145°F (63°C).
4. **Serve**: Slice the pork and serve with steamed rice or grilled vegetables, garnished with sesame seeds.

Hawaiian-Style Pork Tacos

Ingredients:

- 1 lb pork shoulder, slow-cooked or grilled
- 8 small corn tortillas
- 1 cup pineapple salsa (diced pineapple, red onion, cilantro, lime juice)
- 1/4 cup cilantro leaves
- 1/4 cup diced red onion
- 1 lime, cut into wedges

Instructions:

1. **Cook the Pork**: Slow-cook or grill the pork shoulder until tender, then shred it using two forks.
2. **Assemble Tacos**: Warm the tortillas on a skillet or grill. Fill each tortilla with a generous amount of shredded pork.
3. **Add Toppings**: Top with pineapple salsa, cilantro leaves, diced red onion, and a squeeze of lime.
4. **Serve**: Serve with additional lime wedges on the side.

Grilled Mahi-Mahi with Pineapple Salsa

Ingredients:

- 4 mahi-mahi fillets
- 1 tbsp olive oil
- Salt and pepper to taste
- 1 cup pineapple, diced
- 1/4 cup red onion, finely chopped
- 1/4 cup cilantro, chopped
- 1 tbsp lime juice

Instructions:

1. **Prepare the Salsa**: In a bowl, combine the pineapple, red onion, cilantro, and lime juice. Stir to combine and set aside.
2. **Grill the Mahi-Mahi**: Preheat the grill to medium-high heat. Brush the mahi-mahi fillets with olive oil and season with salt and pepper. Grill for 3-4 minutes per side until the fish is cooked through.
3. **Serve**: Top the grilled mahi-mahi with the pineapple salsa and serve with a side of rice or steamed vegetables.

Tropical Fruit Salad

Ingredients:

- 1 cup pineapple, diced
- 1 cup mango, diced
- 1 cup kiwi, peeled and diced
- 1/2 cup papaya, diced
- 1/2 cup coconut flakes
- 1 tbsp honey (optional)
- 1 tbsp lime juice

Instructions:

1. **Prepare the Fruit**: In a large bowl, combine all the diced tropical fruits.
2. **Toss and Serve**: Drizzle with honey (if using) and lime juice, then toss gently to combine. Top with coconut flakes.
3. **Serve**: Serve immediately or refrigerate for an hour before serving for a chilled tropical treat.

Coconut-Lime Chicken

Ingredients:

- 4 chicken breasts or thighs
- 1/2 cup coconut milk
- Zest and juice of 1 lime
- 1 tbsp honey
- 2 cloves garlic, minced
- 1 tsp ginger, grated
- Salt and pepper to taste

Instructions:

1. **Prepare the Marinade**: In a bowl, whisk together coconut milk, lime zest and juice, honey, garlic, ginger, salt, and pepper.
2. **Marinate the Chicken**: Place the chicken in the marinade and refrigerate for at least 30 minutes, up to overnight.
3. **Cook the Chicken**: Grill or pan-sear the chicken for 6-7 minutes per side, or until the internal temperature reaches 165°F (74°C).
4. **Serve**: Serve with rice or a tropical fruit salad, garnished with lime wedges.

Hawaiian Ahi Tuna Tartare

Ingredients:

- 1 lb fresh ahi tuna, diced
- 1/4 cup soy sauce
- 2 tbsp sesame oil
- 1 tbsp rice vinegar
- 1 tbsp honey
- 1 tsp grated ginger
- 1/2 avocado, diced
- 1 tbsp sesame seeds
- 1/4 cup green onions, chopped
- 1/2 tsp wasabi paste (optional)

Instructions:

1. **Prepare the Marinade**: In a bowl, whisk together soy sauce, sesame oil, rice vinegar, honey, ginger, and wasabi paste (if using).
2. **Toss the Tuna**: Add the diced ahi tuna to the marinade and gently toss to coat.
3. **Add Avocado and Garnish**: Carefully fold in the diced avocado and green onions.
4. **Serve**: Garnish with sesame seeds and serve as an appetizer with crackers or on a bed of greens.

Lomi Lomi Salmon

Ingredients:

- 1 lb fresh salmon, skinless and diced
- 1/2 cup tomatoes, diced
- 1/4 cup red onion, finely chopped
- 2 tbsp green onions, chopped
- 1/4 cup Hawaiian sea salt
- 1/4 cup salted or unsalted macadamia nuts, crushed (optional)
- 1 tbsp fresh cilantro, chopped (optional)

Instructions:

1. **Prepare the Salmon**: Dice the fresh salmon into small cubes.
2. **Combine Ingredients**: In a bowl, combine the salmon, tomatoes, red onion, green onions, and macadamia nuts (if using).
3. **Add Salt**: Sprinkle Hawaiian sea salt over the mixture and gently toss to combine.
4. **Chill and Serve**: Let the dish chill in the refrigerator for at least an hour to allow the flavors to meld. Serve with fresh poi or crackers for a refreshing Hawaiian appetizer.

Macadamia Nut Crusted Fish

Ingredients:

- 4 fish fillets (mahi-mahi, tilapia, or snapper)
- 1 cup macadamia nuts, crushed
- 1/2 cup panko breadcrumbs
- 1/4 cup all-purpose flour
- 2 eggs, beaten
- 2 tbsp coconut oil or vegetable oil
- Salt and pepper to taste

Instructions:

1. **Prepare the Coating**: In one shallow dish, mix the crushed macadamia nuts, panko breadcrumbs, salt, and pepper. In another dish, place the flour. In a third dish, beat the eggs.
2. **Coat the Fish**: Dredge each fish fillet in flour, dip it into the egg, and then coat it with the macadamia nut mixture, pressing gently to adhere.
3. **Cook the Fish**: Heat coconut oil in a skillet over medium heat. Cook the fillets for 3-4 minutes per side, until golden brown and cooked through.
4. **Serve**: Serve with a side of tropical fruit salad or coconut rice for a delicious Hawaiian-inspired meal.

Haupia Pie

Ingredients:

- 1 1/2 cups coconut milk
- 1/2 cup sugar
- 1/4 cup cornstarch
- 1/4 tsp salt
- 1/2 tsp vanilla extract
- 1 pre-baked 9-inch pie crust (graham cracker or pastry)
- 1/4 cup shredded coconut, toasted (optional)

Instructions:

1. **Prepare the Filling**: In a saucepan, whisk together coconut milk, sugar, cornstarch, and salt. Heat the mixture over medium heat, stirring constantly until it thickens and comes to a gentle boil.
2. **Cool the Filling**: Once thickened, remove from heat and stir in the vanilla extract. Allow the mixture to cool for 5-10 minutes.
3. **Assemble the Pie**: Pour the coconut mixture into the pre-baked pie crust. Smooth the top and refrigerate for at least 3 hours or until set.
4. **Serve**: Top with toasted shredded coconut before serving for added texture and flavor.

Kona Coffee Rubbed Steak

Ingredients:

- 2 ribeye steaks
- 2 tbsp Kona coffee grounds
- 1 tbsp brown sugar
- 1 tsp smoked paprika
- 1 tsp garlic powder
- 1/2 tsp salt
- 1/4 tsp black pepper
- 1 tbsp olive oil

Instructions:

1. **Prepare the Coffee Rub**: In a small bowl, combine the Kona coffee grounds, brown sugar, smoked paprika, garlic powder, salt, and pepper.
2. **Rub the Steaks**: Pat the steaks dry with paper towels. Rub the coffee mixture evenly onto both sides of each steak.
3. **Cook the Steaks**: Heat olive oil in a cast-iron skillet over medium-high heat. Cook the steaks for 4-5 minutes per side, depending on the thickness and desired doneness.
4. **Serve**: Let the steaks rest for a few minutes before slicing. Serve with mashed potatoes or grilled vegetables.

Spam and Egg Breakfast Sandwich

Ingredients:

- 2 slices of Spam
- 2 eggs
- 2 English muffins, split and toasted
- 1/4 cup shredded cheddar cheese
- 1 tbsp butter
- 1 tbsp soy sauce (optional)
- 1 tbsp mayonnaise (optional)

Instructions:

1. **Cook the Spam**: In a skillet, cook the Spam slices over medium heat until golden brown and crispy on both sides, about 3-4 minutes per side.
2. **Cook the Eggs**: In the same skillet, crack the eggs and cook them to your preference (fried, scrambled, or poached). Season with salt and pepper, and drizzle with soy sauce if desired.
3. **Assemble the Sandwich**: Spread mayonnaise on the toasted English muffin halves (optional). Place a slice of cooked Spam on each muffin, followed by a cooked egg, and top with shredded cheddar cheese.
4. **Serve**: Serve immediately for a delicious and hearty Hawaiian-style breakfast.

www.ingramcontent.com/pod-product-compliance
Lightning Source LLC
LaVergne TN
LVHW061958070526
838199LV00060B/4184